Optical Illusions Coloring Book

30 Amazing Illustrations
That Will Trick Your Brain

www.ColoringCraze.com

Copyright © 2017 ColoringCraze

All rights reserved.

ISBN: 1975600991
ISBN-13: 978-1975600990
Edition: 2

FREE GIFT FOR YOU!

Coloring books enthusiast? Get **Free Bonus Kit** from the site below:

=> http://www.coloringcraze.com/**bonus** <=

WWW.COLORINGCRAZE.COM

WWW.COLORINGCRAZE.COM

WWW.COLORINGCRAZE.COM

WWW.COLORINGCRAZE.COM

WWW.COLORINGCRAZE.COM

WWW.COLORINGCRAZE.COM

WWW.COLORINGCRAZE.COM

WWW.COLORINGCRAZE.COM

WWW.COLORINGCRAZE.COM

WWW.COLORINGCRAZE.COM

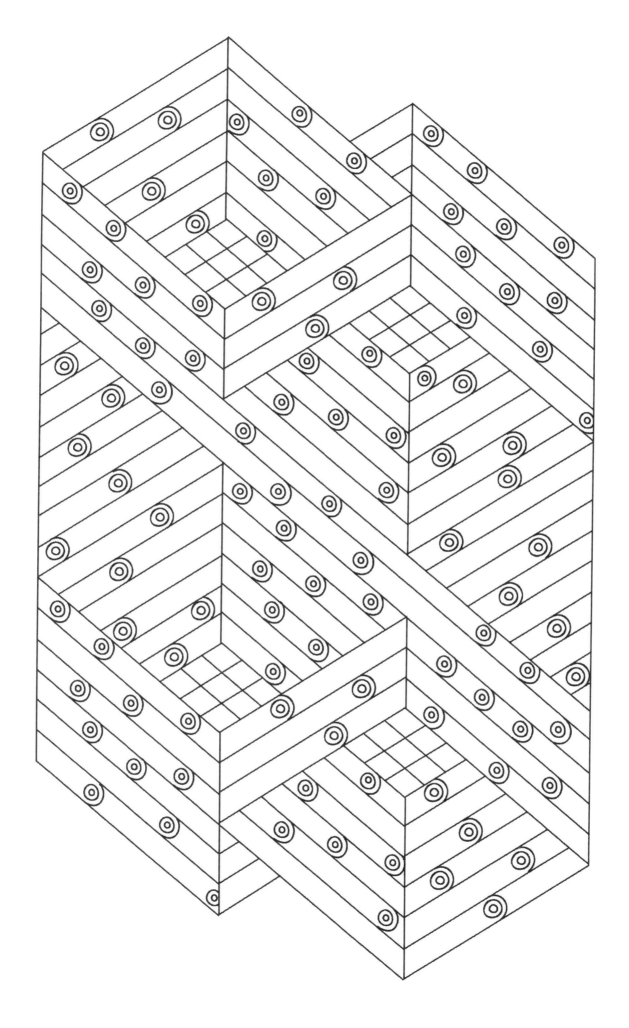

WWW.COLORINGCRAZE.COM

WWW.COLORINGCRAZE.COM

WWW.COLORINGCRAZE.COM

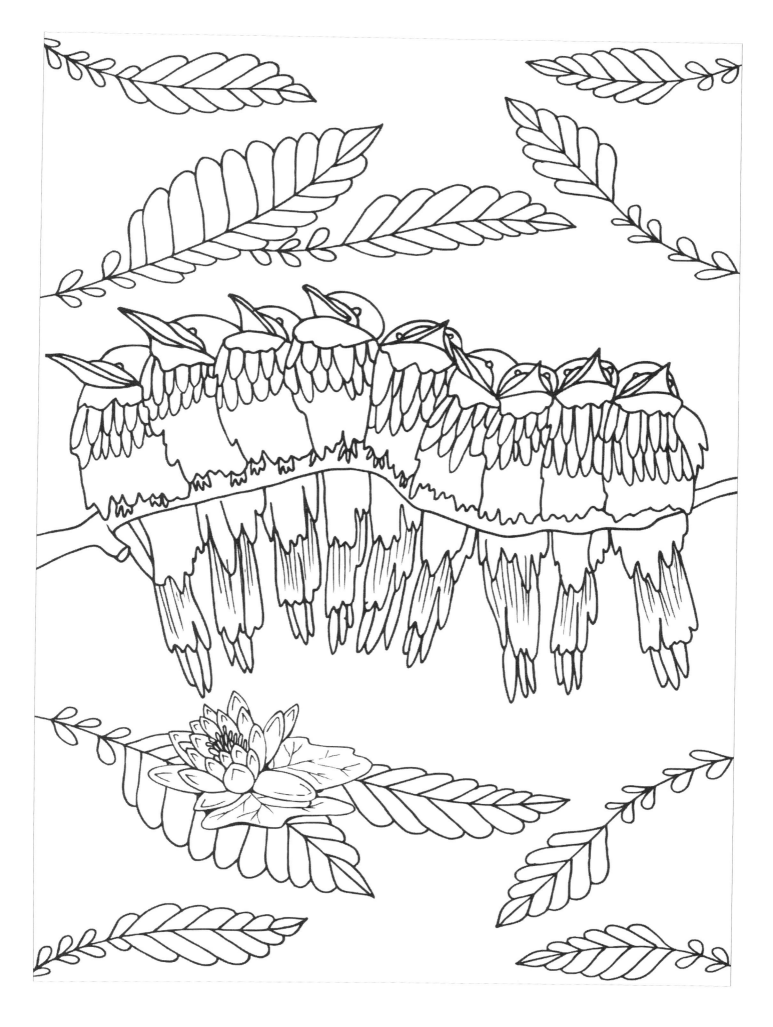

WWW.COLORINGCRAZE.COM

WWW.COLORINGCRAZE.COM

WWW.COLORINGCRAZE.COM

WWW.COLORINGCRAZE.COM

WWW.COLORINGCRAZE.COM

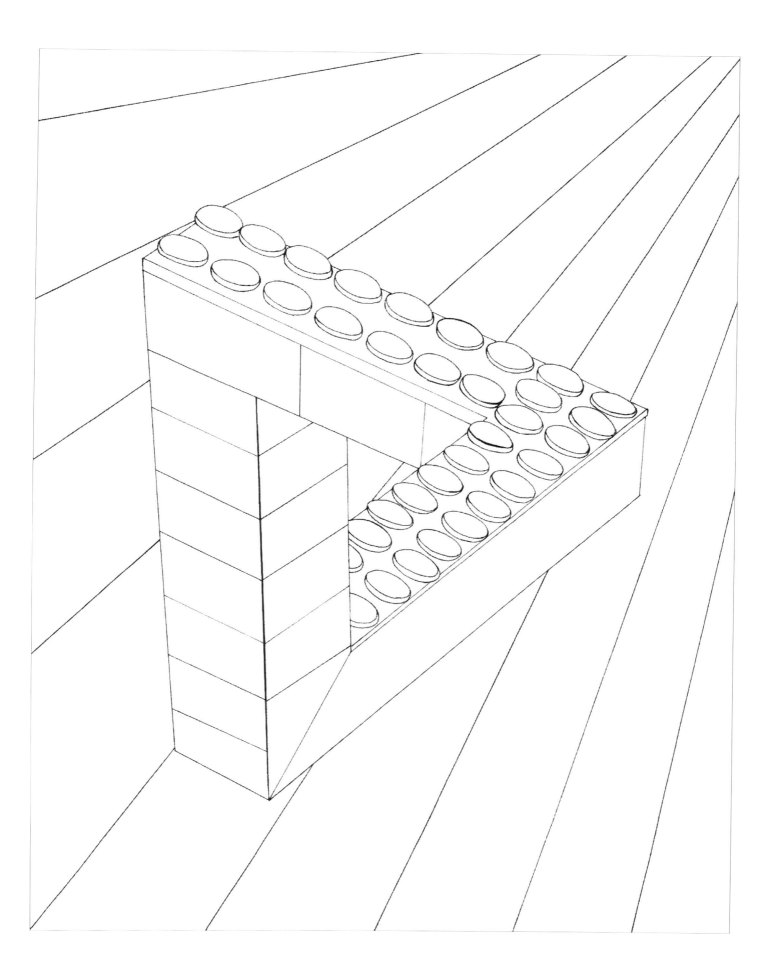

WWW.COLORINGCRAZE.COM

WWW.COLORINGCRAZE.COM

WWW.COLORINGCRAZE.COM

WWW.COLORINGCRAZE.COM

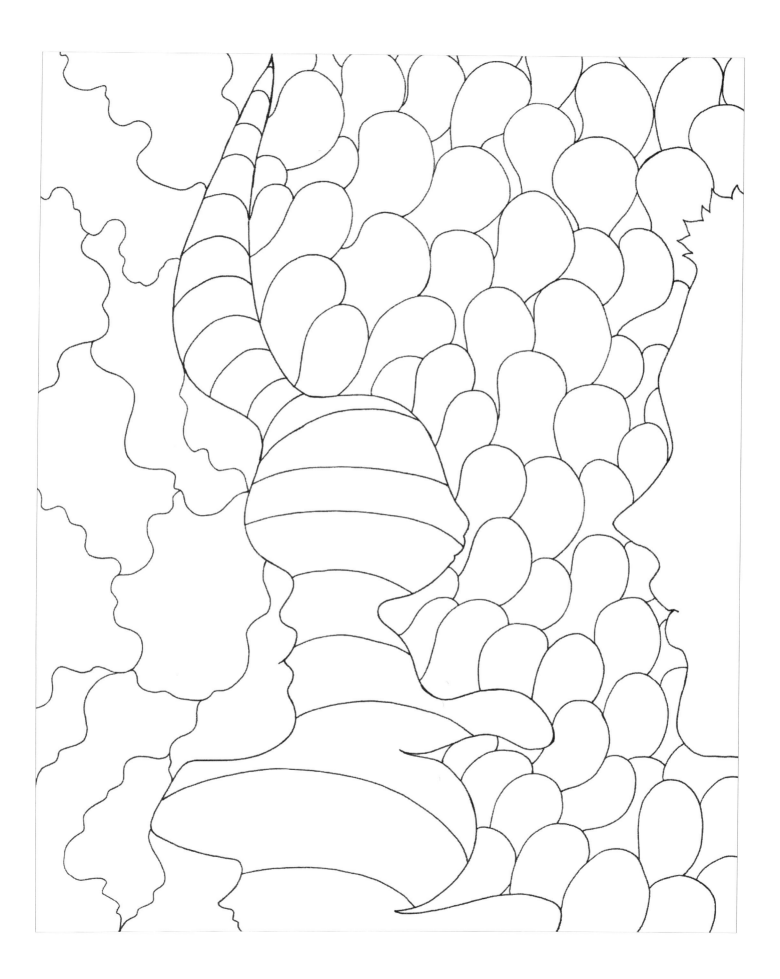

WWW.COLORINGCRAZE.COM

WWW.COLORINGCRAZE.COM

WWW.COLORINGCRAZE.COM

WWW.COLORINGCRAZE.COM

WWW.COLORINGCRAZE.COM

WWW.COLORINGCRAZE.COM

WWW.COLORINGCRAZE.COM

WWW.COLORINGCRAZE.COM

WWW.COLORINGCRAZE.COM

WWW.COLORINGCRAZE.COM

WWW.COLORINGCRAZE.COM

31st Bonus Illustration

WWW.COLORINGCRAZE.COM

FROM THE AUTHOR

Thanks for coloring our book! I hope it was relaxing and I hope you had a lot of fun with it.

I would like to ask you for a *small* favor. Book reviews are very important for other coloring enthusiasts like you. If you have a minute, please leave a comment under our book here: **www.coloringcraze.com/review24**

It will help the buyers to make a decision and your feedback will be priceless to our illustrators ☺

All our other books are available here: www.coloringcraze.com/**our-books**

Remember to grab your **Free Bonus!**

=> http://www.coloringcraze.com/**bonus** <=

Thank You!

Printed in Great Britain
by Amazon